Gideon
Blows the Trumpet

The Word of the King Series

Gideon
Blows the Trumpet

by

Cor Van Rijswijk

Illustrated by Rino Visser

INHERITANCE PUBLICATIONS
NEERLANDIA, ALBERTA, CANADA
PELLA, IOWA, U.S.A.

National Library of Canada Cataloguing in Publication Data

Rijswijk, Cor van, 1939-
  Gideon blows the trumpet / Cor Van Rijswijk, Rino Visser.

  (The Word of the King series)
  Translation of: Gideon blaast de bazuin.
  ISBN 1-894666-22-4

  1. Gideon (Biblical judge)—Juvenile literature. I. Visser, Rino.
II. Title. III. Series.
BS580.G5R5513 2003   j222'.3209505   C2003-910231-9

Library of Congress Cataloging-in-Publication Data

Rijswijk, Cor van, 1939-
  [Gideon laast de bazuin. English]
  Gideon blows the trumpet / by Cor Van Rijswijk ; illustrated by Rino Visser.
    p. cm. — (The Word of the King series)
Summary: A chapter-book retelling of the Old Testament story of Gideon
and the small army God told him to lead against the much stronger and
larger army of the Midianites.
  ISBN 1-894666-22-4
  1. Gideon (Biblical judge)—Juvenile literature. [1. Gideon (Biblical judge)
2. Bible stories—O.T.] I. Visser, Rino, ill. II. Title.
  BS580.G5R5513 2003
  222'.3209505—dc21

2002156699

Originally published as *Gideon laast de bazuin* (1999)
by Uitgeverij/Boekhandel Gebr. Koster, Barneveld, The Netherlands
Published with permission.

Translated by Roelof & Theresa Janssen
Cover Painting and Illustrations by Rino Visser

All rights reserved © 2003 by Inheritance Publications
Box 154, Neerlandia, Alberta Canada T0G 1R0
Tel. (780) 674 3949
Web site: http://www.telusplanet.net/public/inhpubl/webip/ip.htm
E-Mail inhpubl@telusplanet.net

Published simultaneously in U.S.A. by Inheritance Publications
Box 366, Pella, Iowa 50219

Available in Australia from Inheritance Publications
Box 1122, Kelmscott, W.A. 6111 Tel. & Fax (089) 390 4940

Printed in Canada

Contents

The Word of the King Series

Abraham's Sacrifice

Gideon Blows the Trumpet

David and Goliath

Audio recordings of these books
are available on Compact Disc.

Dutch titles are also available from

Inheritance Publications
Box 154, Neerlandia, Alberta Canada T0G 1R0
Tel. (780) 674 3949
Web site: http://www.telusplanet.net/public/inhpubl/webip/ip.htm
E-Mail inhpubl@telusplanet.net

1. There They Come Again

"Flee!
We must flee!
There they come again!"
Full of fear
the people ran away.
Mothers snatched
up their children
and ran away too.

Soon there was
no one in sight;
everyone was in hiding.
Many of the people
hid in caves.

No wonder
they hid,
for the strange
soldiers
were back.

The soldiers
stole everything.
And what they
could not steal,
they destroyed,
or, burned
with fire.

In the distance
there was smoke;
it was rising above the fields,
above the beautiful golden fields
of wheat.
The enemy soldiers
started those fires.
They did it on purpose;
they did not want the people
to grind up their wheat
and make flour.
The enemy soldiers
did not want the people
to make any more bread.
And if there was no bread to eat,
the people would starve to death.

After a while the soldiers
went away again.
The people went back
to their homes,
but the fields were
bare and black.
In some places
smoke was still rising.

The Midianites
and their friends
caused all the pain
and sadness.
The Midianites
were terrible people.

Every year
they came.
The Midianites came
to destroy everything.

2. Their Own Fault

Who were these fathers and mothers
and children who feared the Midianites?
They were called the Israelites,
and the Israelites were the people of God.
Now, the LORD had taken good care of His people,
for they were His children.
He gave them food and drink.
He gave them houses
to live in.
The LORD took better
care of His children
than any earthly father
could do.
But now it seemed that
something had changed.
It seemed that the LORD
was not taking care
of His people anymore!
How could this be?
Something dreadful
had happened:
the Israelites
had turned away
from the LORD.
They began to
serve idols instead.
Idols are images
made of wood and stone.
These false gods cannot hear;

they cannot speak.
Only the living God,
who is always faithful,
is truly a God to Israel.
The people had forsaken the living God.
Finally the LORD said:

"By their wilful choice
They My love rejected;
They ignored My voice.
Israel did not
Heed what they were taught.
They My law neglected."[1]

No, the LORD did not help His people anymore.
Every year the enemy soldiers
came into the land of Israel.
God did not stop them:
that was the punishment for His people.
He was punishing them for their sins.

---

[1] Psalm 81:10 in the rhymed version of the
Book of Praise: Anglo-Genevan Psalter.

3. "LORD, Help Us!"

The LORD saw
that His people
were suffering;
He knew
they were unhappy.
He watched
as they fled
to the mountains.
He heard them
crying out;
He saw tears
running down their cheeks.
And then there
came a change:
He saw that they
were starting
to call out
to Him again.
They were saying:

"O LORD,
Thou art
the true God
of Israel;
wilt Thou not save us again?
Help us, O LORD,
please help us!"

Free Thou us from oppression.
For Thy Name's sake we thus
Pray Thee to rescue us
And pardon our transgression.²

Then the Lord sent a prophet.
The prophet said to God's people:
"It is your own fault
that the enemy comes
into your land every year.
You have disobeyed the Lord!"

---

² Psalm 79:3b from the *Book of Praise.*

4. Too Many to Count

Again there were strangers
in the land of Israel.
The Midianites
were back,
and their friends
were with them.
They gathered
in a big valley
at the foot
of a mountain.
There were many,
many soldiers,
so many they
could hardly
be counted.
Everywhere
they could be seen,
and everywhere
they could be heard.

This time
the Midianites
and their friends
were planning
to stay
in the land of Israel.

They were
planning to make
the Israelites,
the people of God,
their slaves.
Then there would
no longer be
a land of Israel.
Then there would
no longer be
a people of God.
Surely no one
would be able
to chase away
such a strong enemy.

5. Gideon

Gideon was one
of God's children.
One day the Lᴏʀᴅ
appeared to him.
"Gideon," He said,
"you must go
and free My people.
You must help them
drive out the Midianites."
Gideon shook his head.
"O my Lord," he said,
"I am not a strong man.
I am not even a soldier.
I am just a farmer.
And there are so many
Midianite soldiers.
I cannot do it."

But the Lᴏʀᴅ said:
"Do not be afraid, Gideon.
I will help you,
and then
you will be able
to chase
those soldiers away.
I will make sure
you succeed."

Gideon listened
to these words,
and he believed God.

6. A Mighty Army

Gideon blew
the trumpet.
The sound
of the trumpet
carried a message.
It was calling
the people
to come to Gideon,
to help him
fight the enemy.

It was good
to see so
many men coming.
The men knew
their land was in trouble.
They knew
their wives
and their children
were no longer
safe at home.
They knew
they had to help Gideon
fight the enemy.

Before long Gideon
had many men around him.

With this army
he hoped to defeat
the mighty enemy.
Gideon knew
the enemy
was much stronger.
It would be
a difficult battle!

7. Too Many Soldiers

Gideon was ready
to attack the enemy.
But then he heard
the voice of the LORD:
"Gideon, you have
too many soldiers.
Let all the soldiers
who are afraid go home."
Gideon did not understand it.
Even now, the Midianites
were much stronger.
They already had
more soldiers than Gideon.
Did God want him
to attack the enemy
with an
even smaller band
of soldiers?
That would be
a foolish thing to do!

Then the LORD
told Gideon
why He wanted this.
"Gideon,
if you attack
the Midianites
with a strong army,

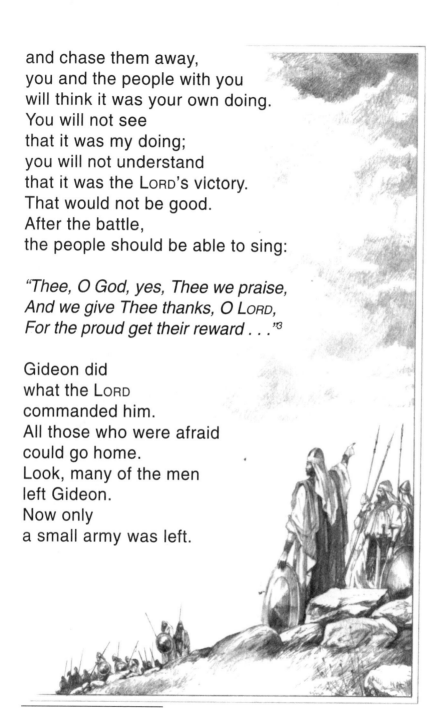

and chase them away,
you and the people with you
will think it was your own doing.
You will not see
that it was my doing;
you will not understand
that it was the L ORD 's victory.
That would not be good.
After the battle,
the people should be able to sing:

"Thee, O God, yes, Thee we praise,
And we give Thee thanks, O L ORD ,
For the proud get their reward . . ."³

Gideon did
what the L ORD
commanded him.
All those who were afraid
could go home.
Look, many of the men
left Gideon.
Now only
a small army was left.

---

³ Psalm 75:1a from the *Book of Praise*.

8. By the Water

Listen!
The LORD
was speaking again:
"Gideon,
take your soldiers
to the stream.
Let each man
drink from the water.
Watch how they drink.
Some will drink
standing up,
but most
will bend down to drink.
Divide the men
into two groups:
the ones
who bend down
and the ones
who stand up."

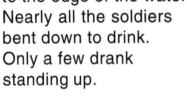

Again Gideon
obeyed the LORD.
He took his men
to the edge of the water.
Nearly all the soldiers
bent down to drink.
Only a few drank
standing up.

Then the LORD
told Gideon
that only the soldiers
who stood up to drink
were allowed to fight.
All the others
had to go home.

Gideon looked
at the men
who were leaving
for home.
Only a small number
stayed with him.
That was the will
of the LORD.

9. A Strange Army

Soldiers carry weapons.
They use them to fight.
In Bible days
soldiers fought
with bows and arrows.
Today soldiers shoot
with guns.
Gideon and his men
had weapons too,
but what strange weapons
they were!
Look at what each man carried.
Each soldier was given
a trumpet to blow on.
And each one carried
an empty jug.
Inside the jug
he had a torch, a lantern.
That is all
the soldiers of Gideon
had with them.
These were
the only weapons
they had.

What a small army!
What strange weapons!

Have you ever heard
of such an army before,
an army
without real weapons?

10. Gideon Is Afraid

Gideon knew he had to fight,
but it would be a strange battle.
He had only
a few soldiers,
and no real weapons.
Yet the LORD gave him
a beautiful promise:
"I will be with you."

Even so,
we read in the Bible
that Gideon
became afraid.
When he thought
about the coming
battle he began
to doubt.
He looked at
the mighty army
of the enemy.
He looked at
his own small army.
He almost
lost all hope.
He thought about
the Midianites.
He knew the enemy
had bows and arrows.

And what did his men have?
Nothing but trumpets
and jugs and torches.
How would he be able
to fight against the Midianites
with such weapons?
Gideon became discouraged.
In his heart he voiced his fear.
He said that the Midianites
were stronger.
How could he attack them
with such a small army?

What a blessing
that the LORD
knew Gideon's heart
and understood his fear.
And so the LORD
comforted His child.
He encouraged Gideon.
The LORD never forgets
His children.

A father with his children sympathizes;
Likewise for us God's pity swiftly rises.
Let all who fear Him in His mercy trust.[4]

Listen!
Once again Gideon heard the voice of the LORD:
"I have given the Midianites into your hands."

---

[4] Psalm 103:5a from the *Book of Praise*.

11. The Dream

It was night.
Slowly, carefully, Gideon crept
toward the enemy camp.
Purah, his servant, was with him.
They were very careful
not to make noise,
for if the Midianites
heard them,
they would be caught
and killed.
Quietly they made
their way forward.

Before long,
Gideon and Purah
entered
the enemy camp.
Most of the
enemy soldiers
were sleeping.
But a few
were awake.
Gideon and Purah
heard voices:
two soldiers were talking.
The two soldiers were in a tent.
Gideon and Purah could hear them clearly.

"I had a strange dream,"
said one of the soldiers.
"I dreamed that
a loaf of barley bread
came tumbling
down the hill;
it tumbled right
into our camp
and struck a tent.
It turned the tent
upside down
and destroyed it."
For a moment
there was silence.
Then the other
soldier spoke.
"Do you know
what your dream
means, my friend?
It means that God
has given us
into the hand
of Gideon.
We will lose
the war against
the people
of Israel."

12. Gideon's Prayer

There was silence
in the tent again.
The soldiers
went back to sleep.
But look,
just outside the tent,
in the darkness
of the night,
there was a man.
Close to the
sleeping soldiers,
Gideon knelt
to praise and thank
the LORD.
"LORD, Thou
hast given me
new courage.
Now I am
no longer afraid.
Thou hast
strengthened me
by this dream.
I thank Thee, LORD!"
Quickly Gideon
and his servant
crept away
from the great camp of the enemy.
They were no longer afraid.

Now they had the courage they needed.
Now they could begin the battle.
The LORD would fight for them
and give them the victory.
They were sure of it.

God, the LORD, is King,
Throned on cherubim.
Let the peoples quake,
Earth's foundations shake.[5]

---

[5] Psalm 99:1a from the *Book of Praise*.

13. A Strange Battle

Before long Gideon
and his soldiers
got ready for battle.
Quietly they advanced
on the enemy camp.
Most of the enemy soldiers
were still sleeping.
A few watchmen
stood guard.
They did not hear
Gideon and his men
approaching.
They did not see the
lighted torches Gideon
and his men hid in their jugs.

Gideon had divided
his small band of soldiers
into three groups.
He told them to do
as he did.
When he blew his trumpet,
they were to blow their trumpets too.
When he broke his jug,
they were to break their jugs too.
And then they would all cry out,
"For the LORD and for Gideon!"
That was all they had to do.

There was no need
to fight the enemy.

Each of Gideon's soldiers
could stay right where he was,
for the LORD Himself
would fight the battle.
Was that not a strange way to fight?

The nations rage, the kingdoms tremble,
The heathen who for war assemble.
When God but speaks, gone is their worth;
His fearful anger melts the earth.[6]

---

[6] Psalm 46:3a from the *Book of Praise*.

14. For the LORD and For Gideon!

Quietly
the three groups of soldiers
surrounded the army
of the sleeping enemy.
It was very, very quiet.

Then, suddenly,
a mighty sound was heard:
it was the sound
of many trumpets!
The noise came
from all around.
And there was still more noise:
Gideon's men
all smashed their jugs.
What a frightening racket
in the middle of the night!

The soldiers of Midian
were filled with fear.
They jumped up.
What was all that terrible noise?
They heard trumpets blaring.
All around them they saw lights.
Where had those lights
come from so suddenly?

Then they began to understand.
They started to realize
what was happening,
for they heard many voices.
The voices were crying out:
"For the LORD and for Gideon!"
The enemy soldiers knew
what this meant:
Gideon had attacked!
In their fear and confusion,
they took their swords
and struck out
at whatever was around them.
But instead of cutting down
the men of Israel,
they began to kill each other.

Gideon and his men
remained where they stood,
blowing their trumpets
and crying out,
"For the LORD and for Gideon!"

15. The Great Champion

The soldiers of Midian
were frightened.
In their confusion
they struck each other
with their swords.
A great many were killed.
A few managed to flee,
but they were caught
by Gideon and his men.

Gideon's small army
had won the battle.
Yet they knew
it was not their doing.
The Lord was
the Great Champion
that day.
It was He
who had won the battle.

Sing to the Lord, a new song voicing,
For mighty wonders He has done.
His right hand and His arm most holy
The victory for Him have won.[7]

---

[7] Psalm 98:1a from the *Book of Praise*.

16. The Battle Continues

Peace returned
to the land of Israel,
and that peace
remained for a long time.
Gideon died,
and now lives in heaven
with the LORD.

Today there is still a battle,
a battle that rages on earth.
That battle
is also being fought
with a trumpet:
the trumpet of God's Word.
The children
and servants of God
are preaching and telling
that Word all over the earth.

Through the blessing of God, people have
repented of their sins and turned to Him.

The ends of all the earth recall His grace
And, turning to the LORD, will seek His face.
All families from every tribe and race
Shall bow before Him.
The kingdoms are the LORD's own habitations
And He alone rules over all the nations;
The proud of heart shall offer invocations
And to Him bow.[8]

---

[8] Psalm 22:10 from the *Book of Praise*.

17. The Last Trumpet

In only a little while
people will hear
the sound
of a trumpet again.
But it will not be
the same trumpet.
It will not be
the trumpet
of God's Word:
no, the trumpet
they will hear
will announce
the day of judgment.
Then the Lord Jesus
will return.
He will come back
on the clouds of heaven.
His enemies
will be destroyed
forever,
but His children
will live with Him
for all eternity.
There will be peace,
and it will last forever.

Let all the streams in joyous union
Now clap their hands and praise accord,
The mountains join in glad communion
And leap with joy before the Lord.
He comes, He comes to judge the peoples
In righteousness and equity;
He will redeem the world from evil
And righteous shall His judgment be![9]

---

[9] Psalm 98:4 from the *Book of Praise*.

Abraham's Sacrifice
by Cor Van Rijswijk

Abraham was rich.
He had many cows and sheep,
donkeys and camels.
He also had lots of gold and silver.
The Lord had given him
all these animals and things.
This book is part of *The Word of the King Series*.
The purpose of this series is to present Bible stories in
such a fashion that young children can read them.
Read them to your four or five-year-old, and let your
six or seven-year-old use them as readers.

Time: Abraham   **Age: 4-8**
ISBN 1-984666-21-6   **Can.$8.95 U.S.$7.90**

2nd Printing

Anak, the Eskimo Boy by Piet Prins

F. Pronk in *The Messenger*: Anak is an Eskimo Boy,
who, with his family, lives with the rest of their
tribe in the far north. The author describes their
day-to-day life as they hunt for seals, caribou, and
walruses. Anak is being prepared to take up his place
as an adult and we learn how he is introduced to
the tough way of life needed to survive in the harsh
northern climate. We also learn how Anak and his
father get into contact with the white man's civilization.
. . This book makes fascinating reading, teaching
about the ways of Eskimos, but also of the power of
the Gospel. Anyone over eight years old will enjoy
this book and learn from it.

Subject: Eskimos / Mission   **Age: 7-99**
ISBN 0-921100-11-6   **Can.$6.95 U.S.$6.30**

2nd Printing

Augustine, The Farmer's Boy of Tagaste
by P. De Zeeuw

C. MacDonald in *The Banner of Truth*: Augustine
was one of the great teachers of the Christian Church,
defending it against many heretics. This interesting
publication should stimulate and motivate all readers
to extend their knowledge of Augustine and his works.
J. Sawyer in *Trowel & Sword*: . . . It is informative,
accurate historically and theologically, and very
readable. My daughter loved it (and I enjoyed it myself).
An excellent choice for home and church libraries.

Time: A.D. 354-430   **Age: 9-99**
ISBN 0-921100-05-1   **Can.$7.95 U.S.$6.90**

William of Orange-The Silent Prince
by W.G. Van de Hulst

Byron Snapp in *The Counsel of Chalcedon*: Here is a Christian who persevered in the Christian faith when the cause seemed lost and he was being pursued by government authorities. Impoverished, he was offered great wealth to deny his principles. He refused. He remembered that true wealth is found in obeying God.

. . . Although written for children, this book can be greatly enjoyed by adults. No doubt Christians of all ages will be encouraged by the life of William of Orange. . . . This book is a great choice for families to read and discuss together.

Time: 1533-1584   **Age: 7-99**
ISBN 0-921100-15-9   **Can.$8.95 U.S.$7.90**

Salt in His Blood
The Life of Michael De Ruyter
by William R. Rang

Liz Buist in *Reformed Perspective*: This book is a fictional account of the life of Michael de Ruyter, who as a schoolboy already preferred life at sea to being at school. . . This book is highly recommended as a novel way to acquiring knowledge of a segment of Dutch history, for avid young readers and adults alike.

Time: 1607-1676   **Age: 10-99**
ISBN 0-921100-59-0   **Can.$10.95 U.S.$9.90**

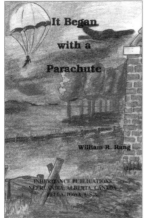

It Began With a Parachute
by William R. Rang

Fay S. Lapka in *Christian Week*: [It] . . . is a well-told tale set in Holland near the end of the Second World War. . . The story, although chock-full of details about life in war-inflicted Holland, remains uncluttered, warm, and compelling.

Time: 1940-1945   **Age: 9-99**
ISBN 0-921100-38-8   **Can.$8.95 U.S.$7.90**

The Tekko Series by Alie Vogelaar

. . . You will watch a little African boy do his utmost to save his little sister. You will see his whole village turn against him. And you will see how God works in wondrous ways to help him. I highly recommend this book for parents to read to their young children, some parts are scary, or for older children to read themselves. — Rebecca Kingswood (*a grade five student*) in *Pioneer*.

Subject: Mission / Fiction   **Age: 8-99**

1 *Tekko and the White Man*	**ISBN 0-921100-47-7 Can.$7.95 U.S.$6.90**
2 *Tekko the Fugitive*	**ISBN 0-921100-74-4 Can.$7.95 U.S.$6.90**
3 *Tekko Returns*	**ISBN 0-921100-75-2 Can.$7.95 U.S.$6.90**

Judy's Own Pet Kitten by An Rook

Fay S. Lapka in *Christian Week*: Judy, presumably seven or eight years of age, is the youngest member of a farm family whose rural setting could be anywhere in Canada. The story of Judy, first losing her own kitten, then taming a wild stray cat with kittens, and finally rescuing the tiniest one from a flood, is well-told and compelling.

Subject: Fiction   **Age: 6-10**
ISBN 0-921100-34-5   **Can.$4.95 U.S.$4.50**

Susanneke by C. J. Van Doornik

Little Susanneke is happy! Tomorrow is Christmas. And Daddy has cleaned the church. But did he forget something? When it is her birthday Mommy always decorates the livingroom. And actually they will celebrate the Lord Jesus' birthday tomorrow. But the church isn't decorated at all. Could the big people have forgotten it? That is sad for the Lord. He loves us so much and now no one has thought about decorating the church for Him. She has to think about that for a moment. What should she do?

Subject: Fiction   **Age: 6-8**
ISBN 0-921100-61-2   **Can.$4.95 U.S.$4.50**

Sing to the LORD
The Children of Asaph
sing the Psalms of David
on the tunes of John Calvin

Noortje Van Middelkoop, Panflute
Lucy Bootsma, Violin
Daniel Bootsma, Cello
Harm Hoeve, Organ
Theresa Janssen, Conductor

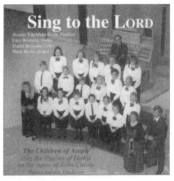

Psalm 42:1, 2, & 5; Psalm 116:1, 2, 3, & 7; Psalm 124; Psalm 1 (Organ Solo); Psalm 49:1 & 2; Psalm 98; Psalm 121; Psalm 96:1, 2, & 8; Psalm 80:1, 2, & 3; Psalm 68 (Organ & Panflute); Psalm 25:1, 2, & 3; Song of Simeon (Hymn 18); Psalm 134.

For all ages!

Compact Disc   **Can.$21.99 U.S.$18.99**
Cassette   **Can.$14.99 U.S.$12.99**

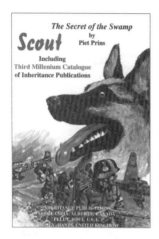

Free copy with first order of any I.P. book!

Scout: The Secret of the Swamp
One of the best stories on the Second World War!

Including the 60 page catalog of Inheritance Publications

Teddy's Button by Amy Le Feuvre

The Life of Faith says: Teddy's Button is by the author of *Probable Sons*, and it would be difficult to say which is the better.

Rev. Thomas Spurgeon says: A smile-provoking, tear-compelling, heart-inspiring book. I wish every mother would read it to her children.

The Christian says: A lively little story, telling of a lad whose military spirit found satisfaction in enlisting in Christ's army and fighting God's battles.

Subject: Fiction   **Age: 8-99**
ISBN 0-921100-83-3   **Can.$7.95 U.S.$6.90**

He Gathers the Lambs
by Cornelius Lambregtse

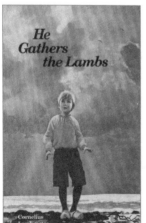

A moving book, written not only with deep insight into the ecclesiastical, religious, social, and historical situation in which the story takes place, but also with a warm, rich understanding of a child's soul. Every page of the book carries proof that it was eked out of the author's own experience. It is written from the inside out, and the people who appear in it are flesh-and-blood people as they walked the streets of southeastern Zeeland. Zeelanders with a mystical character . . . who had great difficulty appropriating in faith the redemptive deeds of the covenant God.

Also beautiful in this story are the descriptions of the natural beauty of the island on which it takes place. The author views nature with a loving but also with a knowledgeable eye. The landscape through all the seasons. . . But what is most striking is his knowledge of the soul of a child, a knowledge born out of love. — Rudolf Van Reest

Subject: Fiction   **Age: 14-99**
ISBN 0-921100-77-9   **Can.$14.95 U.S.$12.90**